MOVE: Adventures at Prosperity Patch

by Kim D. H. Butler
and Spencer Shaw

MOVE: Adventures at Prosperity Patch
Copyright © 2025 Kim D. H. Butler and Spencer Shaw

Prosperity Economics Movement
22790 Highway 259 South
Mount Enterprise, TX 75681
www.ProsperityEconomics.org

First Edition
ISBN: 979-8-9940994-4-5 (paperback)

Produced in the United States of America

Published with the assistance of Social Motion Publishing, which specializes in books that benefit causes and nonprofits. For more information, go to SocialMotionPublishing.com.

Acknowledgments

I love animals; I have had dogs, cats, chickens, pigs, sheep, goats, and dairy cows since 4th grade, and now I have Alpacas! I also love Prosperity Thinking. Now, I am excited to share these loves with children of all ages through my third love: reading! Whether you are an adult or have children, grandchildren, or great-grandchildren, reading with others (and playing games too!) is a fabulous bonding experience, and I am so grateful to the team of Spencer and family for bringing it to your table.

Enjoy, Kim Butler, Mount Enterprise, TX

I grew up hearing stories from my dad and kinfolk which shaped my world today. Sharing stories with kids is a fun way to help them think about big dreams. Huge thank you to my wife for leading our homeschooling and our kids for listening to these stories. A big thank you to Emma for helping Kim and I feel like children again.

We are so grateful to everyone who helps us make this book, like Amanda who leads this project and our awesome designers Cy and Holly.

Spencer Shaw

It was a sleepy morning at Prosperity Patch, but Emma, the wise Great Dane, had a big idea.

"What if we create a special fund that keeps growing and helps us improve the farm over and over?" she suggested excitedly.

The pets gathered around as Emma explained the idea of a Spinning Savings Wheel - It's like a fun game where your money goes around and around, ready to be used whenever you need it!

The other pets listened, intrigued by the idea of money that moves to make things better continuously.

To start their fund, they decided to host a big community fair. "Let's raise some money and then use it to make our farm even better," Emma said, clapping her paws together.

Zippy the rabbit took charge of planning fun attractions,

while Miguel the bull handled all the heavy lifting and organization.

Peanut the cat talked to
vendors to set up stalls,

and Kid the alpaca spread the word to everyone in the nearby town.

Using their savings, the pets set everything up, hoping their investment would pay off quickly.

When the fair day arrived, it was a huge success! The farm was bustling with visitors enjoying games, food, and crafts.

The pets kept track of all the money they made, ready to put it to good use.

After the fair, the first project was to build a beautiful new play area for visitors, which brought even more people to Prosperity Patch.

Next, they gave the barn a coat of fresh bright red paint and fixed the broken fences.

Each project made the farm a little better and brought in more money to keep their funds moving.

However, not everything will always go smoothly. It's important to think carefully about what projects to invest in as sometimes they may not be as successful as we think and that's okay!

As long as we apply what we learn to our next goal, we will be one step closer to being successful.

Over time, as they chose their projects wisely and adjusted their plans, their revolving fund helped the farm flourish.

Prosperity Patch became a wonderful place for both the pets and their visitors, all thanks to the money that kept moving and growing.

Emma's Advice:

Hey there, young dreamer! Think about something you really love or want to improve. Now set a goal for what you need to start or grow your project.

Next, save a bit of your money to reach your goal. Once your project is up and running, you might earn a little extra money. Remember to set aside some of your earnings for future projects, and always keep a little bit for fun! By setting goals and working on small projects, you're learning how to manage your money wisely. Keep dreaming big.

Emma's Questions:

1. What goal could you set to save up for something special at home or in your neighborhood?
2. How could you plan for a special treat and also save some money for a rainy day?
3. If you wanted to buy a toy and also help a friend who needs new crayons, could you split your money to do both?
4. What's a fun project you could start using your money to make someone smile?
5. How would you plan to improve your favorite place, like a park or library?"

A note for your parents!

As our thank-you, the QR code below will give you a valuable white paper focused on Income Strategies at ProsperityEconomics.org/permission.